# GHOST WRITE

# Ghost Writer

Patrick Nobes

Stanley Thornes (Publishers) Ltd

© Patrick Nobes 1989

All rights reserved. No part of this publication may be reproduced or transmitted in any form or by any means, electronic or mechanical, including photocopy, recording, or any information storage and retrieval system, without permission in writing from the publisher or under licence from the Copyright Licensing Agency Limited. Further details of such licences (for reprographic reproduction) may be obtained from the Copyright Licensing Agency Limited, of 90 Tottenham Court Road, London W1P 9HE.

First published in 1989 by Hutchinson Education

Reprinted 1991 by
Stanley Thornes (Publishers) Ltd
Ellenborough House
Wellington Street
CHELTENHAM GL50 1YW
England

98   99   00   /   10   9   8

**British Library Cataloguing in Publication Data**

Nobes, Patrick
　　Ghost Writer
　　I. Title　　II. Spirals
　　428.6

ISBN 0 7487 1022 1

Typeset by Input Typesetting Ltd, London
Printed and bound in Great Britain at Martin's The Printers, Berwick

# 1

'So there it is, Gary,' the boss said. 'I'm sorry but there's no job for you here any more. The office will give you your P45 as you go out. My advice to you is to get down to the Unemployment Benefit Office in the High Street straight away. Then on to the Job Centre. We'll always give you a good reference. Best of luck, and thanks for all you've done.'

Gary felt very bitter about the whole set-up. He'd done a good job, but there was nothing he could do about redundancy. He was out of work. He went to the office and picked up his P45. Then he went to see about Unemployment Benefit and called in at the Job Centre. Nothing.

He managed to walk past the newsagent without going in to buy cigarettes to cheer himself up. No good getting back into that again! Well, at least there was the evening to look forward to. He was going to meet his mates in their local pub, the 'George and Dragon'. Good beer, and tonight there was going to be a gig.

# 2

'Don't look at it like that,' Fred said. He put down the tray with six pints of Hartings Best Bitter on to the table. Gary and his mates were at the 'George and Dragon' waiting for the gig to start. Fred was giving Gary some advice about unemployment.

'Be happy. You're a free man. No boss. Do what you want. Drink up. Here's to your future, Gary.' They all lifted their glasses and drank.

Just then the band came in. There was a burst of loud clapping and whistling. The band grinned and clapped back. Then they started to play.

There were five of them. The drummer had his head shaved with only a green spike of hair left sticking up. There were two men, both with bright red hair, playing guitars. The clarinet player had a beard and was wearing a black hat. He was the oldest person in the band by a good many years. The big surprise was the last person. She was a very dark, very beautiful, tall, slim girl playing a violin. She and the lead guitar shared the vocal work. The band was called *Gut Feeling*.

Gary guessed she was his age, or a year or two older. He couldn't take his eyes off her. And could she play! The band was playing top-of-the-chart stuff mainly. Now and again they'd go into a golden oldie or two. It was in these pieces the girl really got you. She lit the whole band up – and the people in the pub, too.

At the end of the gig, Gary went back to his bed-sit. He had only two thoughts in his mind. One and three-quarters of them were about the girl. The other quarter was about Fred's words: 'You're a free man. Do what you want.' The question was how to stay free. He needed money to stay free. So what could he do? What did he want to do?

He had always had one secret dream. Back at school he had enjoyed only one subject – apart from sport and P.E. He was a great reader, though he didn't tell his mates. He also hadn't told them back in his school days how he spent one or two evenings each week. He'd do his paper round, heat up the tea Mum had left in the micro, then lock himself into his room with his stereo headphones on and write. He wrote stories. Stories about all sorts of things and all sorts of people.

That's how he wanted to earn his crust. He could be free. He could work all day in the bed-sit. He could go to the pub, and gigs or play snooker with his mates a couple of evenings a week. Football at the week-end, and perhaps he'd be able to afford to go and see a film now and again.

It was worth a try. He'd start straight away. He had an old manual typewriter, and he got it out of the cupboard. Instead of going to watch TV on the set belonging to the bloke in the bed-sit next door, he started typing. He was pretty quick. He'd always done the reports for his football teams since his school days. He'd learned from the school secretary, who had given him a few lessons.

He worked late. He got up at his usual going-to-work time and started typing again. By the end of the following day he'd finished his first short story.

# 3

He worked hard, day after day. He was lonely at first. But he saw his mates most evenings. Soon he got used to being on his own during the day.

He found out where the band *Gut Feeling* were playing, and whenever they were doing a gig not far away he went to hear them. He told himself he went for the music, which was good. But deep down, he knew he went because of the girl. The more he saw of her, and the more he heard her playing, the more he wanted to know her.

It was exactly a month since he had started writing. Money was so tight that he had to give up going out most evenings. He couldn't pay for his round in the pub. His friends told him it didn't matter. They would pay. One day, they said, we'll be on the dole, and you'll be working. Then you can buy the drinks.

But Gary stayed in all but one evening that week. The following week he wanted to go and hear *Gut Feeling*, but they were playing miles away. When the day arrived he didn't even have the fare, let alone the two quid entry money.

Then the post arrived. From being at rock bottom, Gary found himself on a high. He opened three envelopes. Inside each was a story he had written. They were being returned.

'The Editor is unable to use this story,' the note with each one said.

The fourth envelope had a cheque in it. A cheque for £100! A magazine was actually going to print one of his stories! He'd be able to buy the drinks this week, and best of all, he could go to the gig that evening.

One other thing he'd promised himself – if he could find the nerve to do it ... 'One day,' he had told himself, 'when you sell your first story, you have got to ask that girl if you can buy her a drink.' Would he have the nerve to ask her that evening?

# 4

The gig was in a pub with a big hall at the back. Gary got there early. He took a seat right next to the platform on which the band would play. He knew exactly where the girl would stand in the line-up. His seat was about two metres away from her.

He'd watched her so often that he knew what she drank in the break. He went to the bar just before the break and bought himself another pint. He got a half for her, in the hope she'd take it when he offered it.

The clapping started at the end of the last piece in the first half. Gary took a deep breath and stepped up to the platform. He held the glass out to the girl.

'Can I give you a drink?' he asked.

She smiled at him. 'Hold on while I put my fiddle away. Then I'll be with you.' She put her violin in its case and turned back to him. Gary led her to his table. They sat down.

'I'm Gary Lyons,' he said. 'And I know from the posters that you are Kate Ashwell. I've heard you play a lot. I think you're very good. I've been hoping to meet you for a long time.'

'I've seen you at some of our gigs,' Kate said. 'We tend to notice blond six-footers who come and listen to us more than once. Good to meet you. Keep on paying your entry money!'

They both laughed. From then on it was easy. They talked as if they'd known each other for years.

The following week Kate had another drink with him at the break. At the gig after that, she looked for him at the beginning. She went over to him and put two pound coins on the table in front of him.

'My round,' she said. 'See you at the break.'

At the break Gary asked her if he could get her a drink at the end.

'Well, I usually have to leave straight away,' she said. 'We all go in the van and get dropped off. The others like to get away as soon as we finish. But I could go home by bus tonight. I don't live far away. Yes, O.K. then.'

As they waited at the bus-stop Gary told Kate about his writing. She told him about her day-time job, and how she wanted most of all to earn her living by playing the violin full-time. The bus came along, and they went up on top. They talked easily and laughed together. Gary wanted the journey to go on for ever. Then his heart missed a beat. Suddenly his happiness disappeared. Kate leaned across to point out the place where she worked. Something flashed on her finger. It hadn't been there before. It was a diamond engagement ring!

She saw the look on his face. They already understood each other so well that he didn't need to say anything. She rested her hand on his sleeve for a moment.

'I'm sorry, Gary. I take the ring off when I'm playing. I should have said. I'm engaged. But I hope we can go on being friends. I enjoy your company. Here's my stop coming up. See you soon, I hope.'

Before he could answer she had squeezed by him, and gone down the steps and left the bus. Gary had hoped to take her to her door. Instead he sat there. All his dreams were smashed.

# 5

He tried to keep away from the next gig. But he couldn't. He sat at the back of the hall. Kate had never played better, or looked lovelier. Gary's heart was as heavy as lead. He nearly left at the break. He saw a man go up to Kate and ask her something. She pointed towards the back of the hall. The man looked where she was pointing, and went off to the bar. Then Kate left the platform and Gary suddenly realized that she was coming to his table. He felt very tense, and knew his hands were shaking.

'Hello, Gary,' she said. 'I'm glad you're here. I want you to meet someone. He's getting drinks for all three of us.'

The man came across the hall carrying a tray with the three drinks on it. Gary guessed that he was Kate's fiancé. He was quite good-looking. A pleasant sort of person. As tall as Kate, but a few inches shorter than Gary. He had brown hair. He was quite well-built, but he stooped a bit and wore glasses. He looked like a man who spent a lot of time with books.

'Gary, meet Vince, my fiancé,' Kate said. 'You know about each other.'

The two men shook hands. Gary felt his stomach turn over. So this was the man Kate was in love with.

'So you're a writer,' Vince said. 'I'm a computer man. Kate

thinks I can help you. Let's go back to my place after the gig. I'll show you what my machine can do.'

The gig was a great success. But Gary didn't enjoy it much. Kate sang and played beautifully. He got a lump in his throat when the band did a number he hadn't heard them do before. It was the old Beatles number 'Yesterday'. Gary guessed that Kate had set it for the band. Her violin part really got at you. When it was her turn to sing, Gary thought of the dreams he had had of the two of them together. All yesterday, now.

At the end of the gig Gary wished he had the will-power to leave them. But he found he would put up with anything to see more of Kate, even if it was torture.

They went back to Vince's place. Vince showed Gary his computers. He had a powerful new one, and a smaller old one that he didn't use any longer.

Vince said: 'Kate tells me that you find the hardest bit of writing is having to type whole pages out again each time you change something. I can see it takes hours. But with one of these things you can easily make any changes you want to. You don't have to type out a whole page again because some of it has had to be changed. Watch this.'

Vince showed Gary how the computer could be used as a word processor. Then Vince asked him about his ideas for his next story.

'They are only ideas,' Gary said. 'I don't know how the story will work out.'

'Just type the ideas on to the computer,' Vince said. 'Type them any old how, in any order.'

Gary typed the ideas and the names of the characters. The plot had no real shape or sense, and no ending. Then Vince fed in a program, and typed 'Run'.

The printer chattered away for about three minutes. It printed from left to right and back again at a very high speed. When it stopped, Vince tore off the long sheet the printer had covered. He gave it to Gary to read. Gary was very surprised by what he read. The computer had put together his ideas in three different ways.

'It's an old program I worked out,' said Vince. 'The computer can't really invent anything. It can only arrange and rearrange ideas in different ways. It took me months to do the program. I enjoyed doing that. I'm not interested in the stories. But you are. If it's any use to you, you can have the program. And you can borrow my old computer. If you get on with it, you can make me an offer for it.'

Gary saw how much time the computer would save him in rewriting and retyping. He wasn't keen on letting it play with his ideas, though. He thanked Vince, and said 'yes' to his offer of the computer and the program.

Then they had some coffee. Kate was very quiet. Vince had hardly stopped talking. He went on and on about his computing. Gary guessed that Kate had heard it all before, and he realized that Vince was a complete bore.

He caught Kate's eye once or twice. All life seemed to have

gone out of her lovely face. She looked very sad. Gary began to worry more about her than about his own unhappiness. He was glad to find an excuse to leave.

Before he went they arranged that Gary would borrow a mate's car to go to the next gig. He would give Kate a lift home, and pick up the computer and printer from Vince's place.

# 6

The evening of the next gig came. Gary borrowed his mate's car. At the end of the gig he waited for Kate. She got into the car and he started off in the direction of Vince's place. He didn't say much. He had thought about Kate all the time since their last meeting. She was such a lively, interesting person. How could she be in love with a bore like Vince? What a waste!

Kate was quiet, too. Then she said: 'Look, Gary, I've got some explaining to do. I owe it too you. Take me to my place first. Drop me off. Go round and pick up the computer from Vince. Then come back and see me. Please don't tell Vince. Just say I was very tired and asked to be taken home first.'

Gary was surprised, but didn't ask any questions. He did as he was asked. He picked up the computer, and left Vince as soon as he could.

It was the first time he had been into Kate's flat. It was warm, homely and clean. Kate gave him an easy chair and some coffee. Then she went straight into what she wanted to say: 'You can't understand why I'm engaged to Vince, can you? He's a dead bore. Well, he wasn't when I met him. He was interested in all sorts of things. He was good fun. He liked my music, and thought I was great. We really were in love.

'Then he started doing more work on his computers. They

gradually took over. Now he can't talk about anything else. I'm keeping with him because I hope I'll find the old Vince again. He must be inside there somewhere.'

Gary didn't know what to say. He felt very sorry for Kate. But he also felt she was wasting her time. He'd met some one-track people before. But Vince was about the biggest bore he had ever met. Gary was ready to bet anything that Vince would get worse, not better.

He sat there in silence. He found himself looking deep into Kate's dark eyes. Suddenly Gary found himself saying: 'You know very well how I feel about you, Kate. I'm sorry about you and Vince. But you can't win. There's no hope for him. I'm sure I could make you happy. I'll be at the next gig. If I've said too much, keep away from me. Thanks for the coffee.'

He got up and went straight out of the flat without saying anything more.

# 7

Gary found the only way he could get Kate out of his head was by working hard. He typed away at the computer keyboard. He turned out perfect copies of stories in half the time that it had taken him on his old typewriter. He sent the stories off to magazines.

Then he got stuck on the next story. He had some ideas, but they wouldn't come together. He got so fed up that in the end he did something he had told himself he would never do. He fed the ideas into the computer, and ran Vince's program.

The printer chattered away. After a few minutes it stopped. Gary tore off the length of print-out. He read the first version of what the computer had written. It was very funny. All the ideas were there. But they had been joined to each other so that they made sense only in a mad sort of way. No help at all.

He went on to the other two versions. They *did* make sense. In fact the last one really got him thinking. He suddenly saw how he could make the best of his story. But he was also very puzzled. In each one of the three versions was an idea that he had not fed into the computer. It was the same idea each time, but used in a different way.

The first version had: 'Hero about to make a great discovery in his laboratory. Gales bring down a tree on his laboratory. All his work is smashed and a great discovery is lost.'

The second version had: 'Hero carrying great discovery in car. Hurricane brings down tree on to road. Car hits tree. Discovery smashed and lost.'

The third version had: 'Girl and hero on boat. He is bringing his great discovery up the Thames to London. 100 mph winds in the Channel wreck boat. Discovery lost.'

Gary had fed in the idea of a great discovery in science. He had a girl and her boyfriend, who was the hero of the story. He had put in a car and a yacht. But he had *not* fed in any mention of hurricanes, strong winds or gales. Perhaps a bit of old memory had not been rubbed off the disc, which was not a new one. But he stopped puzzling about it. There was work to be done.

He wrote all that day and the next to finish the story. Then he posted it to a magazine.

# 8

The following evening there was another *Gut Feeling* gig not far away. Gary went along and got two drinks ready for the break. The band stopped playing. There was loud applause. Kate had shown no sign of seeing him. Two men went up to her. Gary could hardly watch. She was smiling and chatting to them. 'That's it,' he thought. He got up to go. But Kate had left the two men and was coming straight towards him.

'Hello, Gary,' she said. 'I'm very glad to see you. Where's that drink you promised?' She was smiling but her eyes were sad and held his for a long second. They talked in a friendly way during the break, but not as easily as before. At the end of the gig, Kate told the band to go off in the van without her. Gary took her back to her flat. He hoped to be invited in, but Kate stood outside.

'Thanks for seeing me home, Gary,' she said. 'But that's the end of the evening. I don't know quite where I'm going yet. Except that I hope I'll see you again.'

She reached up and gave him a quick peck on the cheek. Then she turned and was gone.

Gary went back to his bed-sit. It was nearly three a.m. before he got to sleep. Partly this was because he kept thinking of Kate. But partly it was because of the noise of the wind roaring round the building. He had never heard such a strong wind before. He was surprised not only at its strength, but also because there had been no gale warnings on the weather forecast before the six o'clock news.

He woke later than usual. As he ate breakfast he switched on the radio. The news was full of the hurricanes that had swept through Britain during the night. Many areas were without electricity. Hundreds of thousands of trees had been blown down. Roads were blocked all over the country. Gary tried to put the storm out of his mind. He got down to work. He cleared the table of the waste sheets of computer print-out left from the last story. He was just going to throw them away when his eye was caught by the words: 'gales', 'hurricane', and '100 mph winds'.

'That's very strange,' he thought. 'Somehow the computer uses an idea I didn't feed into it. Then a few days later something happens that is just like the computer's idea. That would make a good story. I must remember it.'

He started writing again. This time he was trying a sci-fi story. He had several good ideas to put into the story. As soon as he began to puzzle about the best way of using them, he stopped.

'Why worry?' he asked himself. 'Let the computer have a go at it first, this time. It may save me hours.'

He typed the ideas into the machine. Then he fed in Vince's program. The printer chattered away. After a few minutes it stopped. Gary tore off the print-out, and looked at the three versions of his ideas that the computer had turned out.

Once again, he had a good laugh at one of them. It had come out like a mad dream. But the others made a lot of sense. Gary began to make a few notes. Then he stopped as if he had had a shock. He went back over the print-outs. It had happened again.

Amongst all his own ideas a new one had appeared. Not only that, but it was there in all the versions. Gary had fed in ideas about a powerful rocket taking a space craft away from earth. He had put in a crash-landing as the craft reached Mars. What he had *not* put in was an accident when the space craft was taking off from the earth. In all the computer versions, there was a lift-off accident. Gary had not said where the space craft was taking off from. In the computer version, the take-off was from the USA.

'I *must* make sure this disc is wiped clean,' Gary told himself. 'I don't want somebody else's ideas in my stories. I can't have this.'

But he thought it was very strange that a bit of old memory should fit into both of the stories that he'd tried with the computer program. It was a chance in a million.

Gary finished the story in three days. On the day after that there was a dreadful tragedy at Cape Kennedy in the USA. A huge rocket, the first of a new type, exploded on lift-off. All five of the crew were killed. Gary knew that he was no longer dealing with a question of chance.

# 9

A week later, Gary and Kate spent a whole Saturday afternoon and evening together. Before this, Kate had always said no when Gary had asked her out. Kate didn't tell Vince about the Saturday. She wasn't happy about not telling him. But he was even more tied up with his programming. He had gone away on a computing conference for a fortnight.

Above all, Kate found herself getting fonder and fonder of Gary. He made no secret of the fact that he was in love with Kate.

They had a very happy Saturday. They saw a good film in the afternoon. Then they had something to eat in Gary's bed-sit. Then they went to a disco. Afterwards, Gary took Kate back to her flat. It was very late before he left. He'd never been so happy.

They spent nearly all the following weekend together. The only unhappy moments were when Kate thought of Vince. She knew now she couldn't go on with her engagement. Vince was no longer the person she'd said 'yes' to. Anyhow, looking back, she knew now that if she'd had to choose between Vince and Gary at the start, she'd have chosen Gary. They shared more interests than she and Vince had ever done. But she had to be sure. So did Gary. They'd both fallen for people before, only to find that the strong feelings hadn't lasted.

They talked about how and when to tell Vince. They talked about how they could spend enough time together to be sure about things. They had the idea of going abroad for as long as they could afford. They would go back-packing through Turkey. The harder the going, the better they would get to know each other.

The main problem was money. Kate had a good salary and the money from the gigs, but she was paying a high mortgage on her flat. Gary had only just enough to live on. Kate said that she would pay his fare, but he said no, and that he must find his own money. He worked even harder. His real wish was to make enough money to pay for Kate, too.

His next story was about the Stock Exchange. He had been taken there by one of his mates whose father was a messenger. He had spent a whole day there. He'd got talking to a few young men who bought and sold shares, and that had given him an idea for a story.

He made notes on the main characters in the story. He wrote down his ideas about the plot. Then, to see if it would save time, he fed all the ideas into the computer and used Vince's program.

Soon the printer was busy. After a few minutes, the computer's version was ready for him to read. This time he was half expecting the computer to have put in an idea of its own. And he was right. He spotted it straight away.

'Hotel group wants to buy a supermarket chain and offers high price in bid for shares.' 'Keyworth supermarket shares go up in value in take-over bid.' 'Rest House Hotels build an empire.' Three different sets of words for the same idea. Gary had not fed in anything to do with a take-over bid or the high price of shares. He was very excited. When the computer put in the idea of a hurricane, there was a hurricane. When the computer put in a rocket tragedy, there was an explosion on lift-off. Gary felt sure that there would be a take-over of a well-known supermarket chain by a well-known hotel group. The supermarket shares would go up in price. Anyone who owned the shares would be able to sell them and make a lot of money.

The following day he went to everyone he knew to borrow money. He borrowed a tenner here, and twenty there. From one of his mates he even got fifty. He borrowed a hundred off Kate, without telling her why. If all went well, that would be her fare taken care of. If he'd got it wrong ... That didn't bear thinking about.

Then he rang one of the men he had met on the Stock Exchange. He agreed to buy shares in the supermarket chain for Gary.

# 10

For a fortnight the supermarket shares went down each day. Each day their value became a penny or two less. Only a penny or two it was true, but they went steadily down, and every penny was important to Gary. He had promised to pay everybody back in three weeks. He had reckoned it was safe to tell people that. The pieces the computer had put into the other stories had come true within a few days. Gary got more miserable as the days went by.

Then, four days before the three weeks were up, there was a sudden change. The shares went up 20p each. The next day they jumped another 20p. Then on the news there was a ten-second report that Rest House Hotels were making a bid to buy the supermarket chain. The shares went up another 30p. Gary decided to wait to see whether the shares would go up by half the price he had paid for them. If they did, he would make nearly £400. He and Kate had reckoned that they needed £200 each to go on their back-packing trip. £400 profit would pay for both of them.

Three weeks to the day on which he had borrowed the money, the shares hit the price he was aiming at. He sold them immediately. That night he returned the money he had borrowed from his mates.

On the following evening he went round to see Kate. He told her how he'd bought the shares by playing a hunch, and had sold them for a profit. He gave her back her £100 and the extra £50 the shares had made for her.

'And I'm paying £50 more than you towards the holiday,' he said. 'No arguments. You've got the hard bit, deciding what to do about Vince. This is all I can do to help.'

Kate went to see Vince that evening to tell him how she felt, and that she was going to Turkey with Gary. Later, when Gary rang her from a phone box, Kate didn't sound too upset. She sounded puzzled.

'I don't know how he took it, Gary,' she said. 'I began to tell him about us. He just said that he had a good idea that's how things were. He didn't seem surprised when I told him we were going to Turkey. He didn't seem to be jealous or angry, just a bit sad. When I talked about ending the engagement, he said to wait until we got back, and to see then. The end was the strangest bit. He sort of wandered over to the computer. He said goodbye as he sat down. He looked as if he was miles away. It was creepy. I don't think he can take his mind off the computer programs these days. Anyhow, I left. It wasn't anywhere near as bad as I thought it was going to be.'

# 11

The plans for the back-packing were soon made. Kate and Gary found that they could get very cheap one-way air tickets to Turkey. They decided to fly out and then make their way back across Europe on cheap coaches.

They spent the evenings together working out their route. They read as much as they could about the places they hoped to go to. They decided to take one personal stereo between them and six tapes each. They took two books each, of a sort they both enjoyed. A lot of things from their first lists had to be left out when they came to packing their rucksacks, but in the end they finished.

A friend of Kate's was taking them to Gatwick. The plane left at five thirty a.m., and they would have to leave at three a.m. for the airport. Gary thought there wasn't much point in going to bed on the last night, so he decided to work until three a.m. Their plans for the trip, and their growing happiness together had given him an idea for a love story. He wanted to get the main ideas for the story down on paper before they left. He had seen how the story would start. The middle bit was clear, too. He finished that bit about midnight. But he was stuck over the end of the story, and he was getting tired. He thought he'd let the computer have a go. He began to feed in the main ideas of the story. It took him about twenty minutes to do. His eyes felt very heavy. He leaned back in his chair to rest them for a few moments. He would just close them while the print-out of the computer's versions came up.

He woke with a start. He looked up to see Kate standing at the open door of his bed-sit.

'Come on, Gary,' she said. 'We're late. You've been asleep. I *told* you to go to bed for a couple of hours and set your alarm.'

Gary jumped up. 'Switch the computer off for me, please, Kate,' he said. 'I've just got to pack my washing and shaving stuff, and then that's everything.'

Kate switched the computer off. She didn't bother to look at the print-out, and Gary didn't have time. They carried his rucksack through the door. Gary locked up. They went quickly down the stairs and into the car.

The print-out hung down over the edge of the table.

# 12

Kate and Gary enjoyed a wonderful time in Turkey. They walked miles through the mountains. They swam in hot springs. They saw beautiful ancient ruins. They ate and drank very well for very little money. Sometimes they had to sleep rough, and were very cold in the early hours of the morning. On some days they had to walk too far, and their rucksacks felt like ton weights. At times their shoulders and feet were burning sore. At times they were lost, hungry and very thirsty. They laughed through it all. Every day made them happier in each other's company. They knew for certain now that their feelings for each other would last.

They were making their way back to Istanbul as the days began to run out. One evening they had been trying for over an hour for a lift, but with no luck. There were very few cars or lorries on the road. They took fifteen minute turns doing the thumbing. While one was thumbing, the other sat on the rucksacks and read. They were too tired to walk any further. It was beginning to get dark.

It was Kate's turn for the thumbing. Nothing went by in the right direction for five minutes. Then they saw a car in the distance, its side-lights showing up brightly in the evening light. Another vehicle was coming in the opposite direction. Kate raised her thumb and waved it at the car. Gary looked up from his book to see if Kate was going to have any luck. He saw that the vehicle coming in the other direction was a lorry. The driver of the car suddenly put his headlights full on to get a better view of the hitch-hikers. The driver of the lorry coming in the other direction was annoyed by the sudden beam of light. He put his headlights full on to main-beam. The driver of the car was blinded for a moment by the lorry's lights. He couldn't see where he was going. He swerved just as he came up to Kate.

He hit her full-on. There was a dreadful crunch of flesh and bones being smashed. Her broken body was lifted into the air.

Gary ran to her. She was already dead. He picked her up in his arms. He sat down holding the blood-soaked body close to him. His head bent over her and he kissed her as if his kisses could make her better. The tears ran down his cheeks. Great sobs shook his body. He was still sitting holding her close when the ambulance and doctors arrived. He would not let her go. They let him carry her into the ambulance and hold her all the way to the hospital in Istanbul.

# 13

Gary's elder brother and Kate's parents flew out together to bring Kate's body and Gary back. Gary's doctor would not allow him to go back to the bed-sit. He stayed with his brother. For a week after the funeral, Gary did not say a word to anyone. He sat looking into space.

The weeks went by. Bit by bit Gary got over the shock, but his deep sorrow remained. At last he began to feel that he wanted to write again, and the doctor said he could go back to his bed-sit. He nearly broke down when he went back for the first time since they had set out together. All the memories came rushing back. His brother comforted him as best he could. He gave Gary a sleeping tablet and sat with him until he went to sleep.

Gary had made up his mind to start work on the following morning. He got up and had breakfast. Then he went over to the computer to start on a new story. He noticed the print-out hanging over the edge of the table. It was the print-out that had been running on the last night before they went to Turkey. He had fallen asleep on that last night and that had made him late. He had rushed out and had not had time to read the print-out before they left for Gatwick. He had forgotten all about the print-out until he saw it again that morning. Now there was plenty of time to read it. Kate wouldn't be coming in to wake him up and tell him to hurry up.

He tore off the print-out and began to go through the versions the computer had come up with. He forced himself to read the story, which was about a couple spending a happy holiday together. He had got the idea from the plans that he and Kate had made. The great wave of sorrow hit him again. Then he saw that the computer had once more put something of its own into the story.

There were three versions of the story. But each one ended in the same way – with an idea Gary had not put in: 'Cars kill both the man and the woman.'

The full horror hit Gary a few moments later. If he had stayed awake on the night they caught the plane, he would have read the print-out. And if he had read the print-out, he could have saved Kate's life. He would have seen the idea that the computer had put in. He would have known that it would come true. The tears ran down his cheeks again as he began to blame himself for Kate's death. It was as well that Gary's brother called in at that moment. He was on his way to work, and decided to check on how Gary was.

Gary told him the whole story. His brother took Gary back to his home, and stayed with him all that day and the next.

'You can't blame yourself, Gary,' he kept telling him. 'Road accidents are always happening. Anyhow, the computer was wrong. You weren't *both* killed. And it was only *one* car, or one car and a lorry, if you think both vehicles had a part in the death. Look, Gary, the computer did *not* know what was going to happen. It can't know things like that. It can't *know* anything. It's only a machine. Anyhow, things didn't happen in the way the computer said. It's a lot of nonsense.'

Bit by bit the argument got through. Slowly Gary was able to face life again.

# 14

A few months later, a couple of Gary's mates said they were going on a cheap skiing holiday. They asked Gary to go with them. They liked his company, and they wanted to cheer him up.

Gary said he would think it over. As he thought about going with them, he got an idea for a story about skiing. He began to put the story into some sort of shape. He couldn't get the end straight. He did something he had not done for some time. He fed the ideas into the computer, and used the program. When the printer stopped, Gary tore the long sheet off and began to read it. He looked to see whether the computer had put in anything of its own. It had.

'He skied hard to escape the avalanche. The snow overtook him,' said one version. 'They dug him out dead. Blond head stained with blood,' said the second version.

Gary sat quietly and thought. He was certain that the computer was forecasting his death. It was warning him that he would die under the snow and ice. But he didn't really want to live. Again and again he had wished that he had died with Kate. He would go skiing with his friends. He would enjoy it because he knew that he would die in an avalanche. He was sure that the computer was right, and that it would happen. His sorrows would soon be over. The guilt he still felt for Kate's death would be over. He would not be taking his own life. He would just be letting things take their course.

He knew his mates would be in the pub. He decided to go and tell them that his answer was 'yes'. He put his coat on. He looked back at the mantelpiece. His big photo of Kate smiled at him. Her face was beautiful and full of life. He smiled back. 'See you soon, Katie,' he said.

He went downstairs and into the street. Kate's smile stayed with him. The wind was very cold. He put his hands in his pockets, and pulled his collar up round his ears. He went on, deep in thought. His steps got slower and slower.

'Is this what Kate would really want me to do?' he asked himself. He knew the answer. She would want him to go on living. She would want him to find the courage to make a success of his life. She wouldn't want him to go on being deep in sorrow because of her death. She wouldn't want him to go on to his own death if he could stay alive.

She was right. He must fight against taking the easy way out. Somehow he must find the strength to tell his mates that he would not be going on the skiing holiday with them. He had to face life, put the past behind him, and get on with things. His mind was made up.

He had come to a stop as he was thinking so deeply. Now he stepped forward. The driver of the car didn't stand a chance.

'He was standing still on the kerb,' the driver told the policeman a few minutes later. 'Then suddenly he stepped out in front of me. I hit him before my foot reached the brake pedal.'

Gary's mate, Fred, had seen it from the other side of the road. He had seen Gary standing there. Then it was just as the driver of the car had said.

Gary was dead by the time they got him to hospital. The doctor looked closely at the bruised face. It should have been twisted up in pain. Instead it looked peaceful. There even seemed to be a gentle smile on the young man's lips.

# The Spirals Series

## Stories

**Jim Alderson**
Crash in the Jungle
The Witch Princess

**Jan Carew**
Death Comes to the Circus
Footprints in the Sand

**Barbara Catchpole**
Laura Called
Nick

**Susan Duberley**
The Ring

**Keith Fletcher and Susan Duberley**
Nightmare Lake

**John Goodwin**
Dead-end Job
Ghost Train

**Paul Groves**
Not that I'm Work-shy
The Third Climber

**Anita Jackson**
The Actor
The Austin Seven
Bennet Manor
Dreams
The Ear
A Game of Life or Death
No Rent to Pay

**Paul Jennings**
Eye of Evil
Maggot

**Margaret Loxton**
The Dark Shadow

**Patrick Nobes**
Ghost Writer

**David Orme**
City of the Roborgs
The Haunted Asteroids

**Kevin Philbin**
Summer of the Werewolf

**Julie Taylor**
Spiders

**John Townsend**
Back on the Prowl
Beware the Morris Minor
Fame and Fortune
Night Beast
SOS
A Minute to Kill

**David Walke**
Dollars in the Dust

## Plays

**Jan Carew**
Computer Killer
No Entry
Time Loop

**Julia Donaldson**
Books and Crooks

**John Godfrey**
When I Count to Three

**Nigel Grey**
An Earwig in the Ear

**Paul Groves**
Tell Me Where it Hurts

**Barbara Mitchelhill**
Punchlines
The Ramsbottoms at Home

**Madeline Sotheby**
Hard Time at Batwing Hall

**John Townsend**
A Bit of a Shambles
Breaking the Ice
Cheer and Groan
Clogging the Works
Cowboys, Jelly and Custard
The End of the Line
Hanging by a Fred
The Lighthouse Keeper's Secret
Making a Splash
Murder at Muckleby Manor
Over and Out
Rocking the Boat
Spilling the Beans
Taking the Plunge

**David Walke**
The Bungle Gang Strike Again
The Good, the Bad and the Bungle
Package Holiday